I0841024

WE'RE NOT ALL ONE

by Karen Kellock Ph.D.

Manual for Superior Men

A complete theory based on Einstein physics,
Political Psychology, Systems Theory
and Archetypal Psychiatry.

FORMULA

All success attraction
All disease obstruction
All recovery elimination

You must fast on all three

OBSTRUCTIONS:

People
Habit
Food

WE'RE NOT ALL ONE

While the herd runs off the cliff, think for yourself and ignore this rift. God categorizes sinners from stars: All who want Satan, go there, all who want Me, be here.   God's giving them enough rope so they feel invincible then their mental illness comes out.   Females tend to get their opinions from The View, neighbors and friends--these are dangerous trends.   Buzzwords: disturbing", hater, homophobe, racist, sexist--these are the words of the anarchists.   In Liberalism there is no crime or punishment: letting violent felons go is our predicament.

WE'RE NOT ALL ONE

HERDS RUN OFF CLIFFS TOGETHER
FEMALES GET OPINIONS FROM THE VIEW
WHAT IS MADE IS TWO, NOT ONE
THE LIE IS SELF-JUSTIFYING
LIBERALS: AN UPSIDE DOWN UNIVERSE
ILLOGIC RULES WITH LIBERAL FOOLS
HATRED OF OUR PRESIDENT: A FIRST
IT'S ALL ORCHESTRATED
THE LAWLESS LOVING SIXTIES
OLD FASHIONED AMERICA BRINGS US UP, NEW AGE DOWN
INCOMPETENCY AND ABUSE: LIBERAL OBTUSE
WE HATE EACH OTHER: STRICT DIVIDE
PATHOLOGICAL ALTRUISM AND VIRTUE-SIGNALING
THE CRAZY SAY DON'T FEAR
CULTURALLY-APPROVED SINS
THE TERRIBLE GROWING TYRANNY
WE WANT FREEDOM, NOT ENVYIN'
LIBERALS CAN'T SEE CYCLES IN HISTORY
BRING IN RADICALS TO ATTACK US
DUMBED DOWN MEANS DANGEROUS
DENY CLIMATE, LOSE GUN RIGHTS
CONSERVATIVES ARE INDIVIDUALS
TOLERANCE HAS LOST MEANING
WITH DONALD WE RETURN FROM THE BRINK
LIBERAL MEANS GROSSNESS
FAKE NEWS LIES
TRUST VERY FEW
MENTALLY ILL WOMEN POWER-TRIPPIN'
OFFICIOUS DOCTOR'S QUESTIONS
CONSTRAIN ENTERTAINMENT
OBFUSCATION NO TRANSPARENCY
MORALITY MADE AMERICA GREAT
BACKGROUND CHECKS LEADS TO CONFISCATION
LIBERALS SIX TIMES MORE LIKELY TO STEAL

WE'RE NOT ALL ONE

False Cosmology Caused Ruin

HERDS RUN OFF CLIFFS TOGETHER

The herd runs off the cliff. Think for yourself and ignore this rift.

God categorizes us, sinners from stars: All who want Satan, go there. All who want Me, be here.

God's giving them enough rope so they feel invincible then their mental illness comes out: have hope.

After Hollywood bewitched the world many are parting from this falsehood, coming back into the fold.

FEMALES GET OPINIONS FROM THE VIEW

Females tend to get their opinions from The View, neighbors and friends--these are dangerous trends.

Buzzwords: "Disturbing", hater, homophobe, racist, sexist--these are the words of the anarchists.

FOX is flooded with leftism under the guise "fair and balanced" but I'm sick of this with no letup.

"Global Warming" is a scam and power grab to take over the energy industry and it means money.

In Liberalism there is no crime or punishment so him letting violent felons go is our predicament.

WE'RE NOT ALL ONE

Cosmology of the bible is separation. Father is separate from children: he punishes but blesses again.

The confrontation is between two world views.

The only solution to modern misery is the biblical worldview of God vs. creation.

Twoism: We have the wisdom of God as a totally separate being from the things He made.

The most profound truth of this generation: God is separate from His creation.

WHAT IS MADE IS TWO, NOT ONE

What is made must be two, not one.

Oneism is an all-inclusive self-justifying cosmology: "personal empowerment" and "human flourishing".

Oneism completely leaves God out--not "individual empowerment" but repentance than God's blessings on man: awed.

No longer called "new age" they just say "I'm spiritual but not religious".

Oneism is "a theory about everything".

Oneism understood: any notion of sexual morality must go, all sex is good.

Oneism comes over youth as a totalitarian coherent system. Oneism is all bull—"not two"—its just Hinduism.

Twoism is the key to the cosmos everywhere but especially sexuality.

Young people's questions are not answered, for example about transgenders. It's not in the bible just paganism sir.

Born this way--an original sin DNA? Accept but don't approve, for homosexuality results from the fall, ok?

WE'RE NOT ALL ONE

Their self-identifications make no biblical sense. If you buy into it you'll never get to your next place and stay dense.

Cure for the mentally sick: a deeply bible-saturated apologetics.

Non-gender clothing: "pure expression of self".

THE LIE IS SELF-JUSTIFYING

The only answer to a self-justifying all-inclusive cosmology based on the lie of oneism is the Truth.

Paganism in the elites produces degraded results in the race. The oneist is overwhelmed by self-will, dis-grace.

The wise are intimidated by all-is-one politically correct thinking but the church is degrading.

Give em the tools to analyze what's happening in the church, to use twoism the solution that works.

Our universities have abandoned all reason to be politically correct--can you imagine that?

University says: Ideas should not be debated but repressed and the True Self never expressed.

The Clintons have turned the politics of personal enrichment into an art form for themselves. Trump

Willfully and eagerly sacrificing everything on the altar of "diversity" and "inclusion": this is confusion.

Trump knows how to show power and no one else does. it can't be faked: it's innate in the high crust.

If these social justice warriors take over we'll be dragged from our homes at night: a blight.

One wonders if he'll have enough time to turn it all around. The devil's working so fast, a siren sound.

WE'RE NOT ALL ONE

LIBERALS: AN UPSIDE DOWN UNIVERSE

With liberals in control it's an upside-down universe. Cronies aren't punished while we are cursed.

With liberals in control we put up with so much crap. Every day it's a new shoe to drop, a new map.

Why do liberal cities become stinking fetid rat holes? Crime/scams, you know.

Extremism in defense of liberty is no vice. Barry Goldwater

Freedom only comes from the clenched fist of truth. NRA

California's soft-on-crime mentality made us a victim and it's the same in all liberal cities and towns.

The left wants to suicide the country cuz they want Cloward and Piven [they don't want prosperity].

They wanna wreck it all to rebuild it but it never happens that way as they sink in their swill/ruin it.

Democrats look at the constitution as evolving through time while to Reps it's eternal foundation sublime.

We are non-suicidal, non-nihilist, common sense constitutionalists.

All logic is gone, now everything's by rote: Stuff they've contrived while they boast.

With liberals in control there is no justice. As God's main attribute, of course this disgusts us.

Did they purposely not do a good job for you cuz you're conservative? Please think about this.

Why did they distress us? Because they were liberals of course.

Outa California liberal hell! The Utah kids are so nice and you never have to tell em twice.

WE'RE NOT ALL ONE

ILLOGIC RULES WITH LIBERAL FOOLS

Whenever liberals are in control illogic rules and they think it's cool as we're dictated to by fools.

Feminism made men the adversary--but protection from a good man is your only hope missy.

How to get through the latter days: Do your own thing--what you're born for--before it's too late.

Dogs sense weakness and people do too. How people act before you get strong is what pushes you.

It's the Fallen Hero Syndrome: When hero slips they all jump on the bandwagon and pull him down.

The most intelligent are really bashed in this generation as the dumbed are compelled to aberration.

It's sick--the bathrooms and everything. The break from norms is all paganism even joyless flings.

Alex Jones is a leading genius of this generation. His glib takes on history and theory: wow, inspiration.

The Washington Post now writes the hit piece talking points for the rest.

The hypocrisy, arrogance and totally delusional behavior characterizes fools going down, yes sir.

They believe in their desperateness if they throw each other overboard they will survive, no jive.

Fake Media is hated so much nothing they can do will ever put Humpty Dumpty together again.

The crazy Hillary/Pelosis are on fruitcake level power trips. So arrogant, mentally ill and fallen: ick!

WE'RE NOT ALL ONE

With this kind of weakness, evil blindness and deadly ignorance the whole world is laughing at us.

I pray the old American spirit explodes as we fight the animating contest of liberty from toads.

HATRED OF OUR PRESIDENT: A FIRST

They want to see their own president as a failure--how pathetic they are!

CNN overnight has a one-star lower-than-cable rating cuz they said our great president was failing.

People across the world are so sick of teleprompters and news garbage/slurs.

Since tyranny is the default setting in mankind, resistance is the animating contest making us divine.

CNN is a filth hole with toilets overflowing. God always reveals things eventually--isn't it interesting?

They ended free speech in the name of not stirring them up: how globalists used Islam nonstop.

He's a tool for the democrats and the radical left. That's Paul Ryan a "republican" but a dirty rat.

Liberal logic can make you hazy but recall that Einstein said "am I, or all the others crazy?"

President Trump is a reprieve like Jonah being sent to Nineveh to give them a chance to repent.

Hillary would've been the end of free speech: mass arrests/huge wars making Hitler look tame.

People who hate Trump are the ones destroying us--treasonous chumps.

In a reprieve God gives nations time to repent--cultural psychology moves as a unit and slowly ascends.

WE'RE NOT ALL ONE

In the times of Noah people were evil cuz they swam in evil waters, no?

This radical ideology is virulent, violent and seductive to millions of people (so we must fight it).

Societies go crazy en masse. It's pure groupthink [cultural psychology] that creates the ass.

I'm done posting the hellish headlines. I may have only a few days left and this time is mine.

After not seeing FOX for two months I saw it today but walked away cuz the urgent was downplayed.

They don't enforce, they complete the smuggling process. Everything's backward, a mess.

We will not find salvation with the controlled left as they've stolen the renaissance to destroy it.

Hillary says it's white folk's fault this happened. So no blame for going out and randomly killing em.

"We need to reform the police" as if it was their fault they got killed. People: think, please!

When you target groups for killing, you're organizing terrorist attacks: these times are chilling.

We can't fight it when the public is so dumbed down. Alex Jones

Black males: The book gets thrown at em and they go to criminal school, lose power and family.

IT'S ALL ORCHESTRATED

This is orchestrated to send em out in the streets to bring in federalization desired by the elite.

Someone should've thrown tomatoes at a despicable performance of a race baiting president.

WE'RE NOT ALL ONE

Too often we judge others by their worst examples and ourselves by our best intentions. George W. Bush

She wrote "all lives matter" but then quickly deleted it. J-LO wants approval, can you believe it?

Race relations were very good before Obama took office. He triggered all of it, plus he's lawless.

It's been hell under Obama. Under this Marxist many got crazy, just gave up or got drunk/lazy.

The precariat is the new dangerous class. Monthly saved from poverty they vote for high tax.

"For the health of the mother" happens 2% of the time yet is used as excuse to abort 98% of the time.

Trump was the heavy while she resorted to tired, hollow platitudes and empty cliches with arrogant attitude.

Liberals are so dense their only concern is words not actions: "Trump's mean"/ignore destruction.

They're so arrogant in their emptiness, so haughty and superior and we're sick of this (soon we'll be outa this).

Gun Control Levels: 1. Increase background checks. 2. National registry. 3. Limit # of guns. 4. Confiscate guns/ammo.

THE LAWLESS LOVING SIXTIES

The loving lawless sixties produced a bunch of old hippies who became unloving tyrannies.

The maximum tyranny is the level you'll accept, for once they get power you won't be able to object.

It's the in-thing to be lewd. It has no class, they're an ass, but it's social acceptance, alas.

WE'RE NOT ALL ONE

Of course they're mentally ill, having bought that line. It's intended to do us in/make us unrefined.

If they can ban anything they can ban everything. Stop giving into brainless kids you're enabling.

They paid two million to teach em how to throw fits about phantom racism that doesn't even exist.

It gives me pleasure to see liberal professors face to face with the monsters of which they're the creators.

Donald is a breath of fresh air. He wants to revive us--defend us--but not for money, he really cares.

We love the Donald cuz he rings a bell. He's obviously the only one who will end this hell.

Upstarts who arrogantly come against Donald, making fools of themselves; mental dwarfs.

The prayer of one good man changes a nation--that's what the bible says, so get prayin'

The general public is so far removed from reality and history they could never understand this tragedy.

Your progeny are empty, worldly and misguided. Feminism--give me a break-- they are not unique, freaks.

I learned the safest place was So. Utah or N. AZ. Looked for a house in that area- -bingo, up came the best.

When there's so much happening just listen to Trump. He is true reality not a bunch of bunk.

OLD FASHIONED AMERICA BRINGS US UP, NEW AGE DOWN

The new age has brought us down while the old fashioned America aspired to be on top, renowned.

WE'RE NOT ALL ONE

Like Nineveh, we could be reprieved! God was to judge, but changed His mind when they believed.

Although a psychologist I have a master's in political science, it's fascinating to me: Political Psychology.

Most women don't study--they get their views from "The View" and crap like that: brainwash and silly chats.

Climate Change is an anti-human shutdown program for austerity--a weapon to cut off our energy.

GE's economic warfare 101: Shut down all competition so they can jack up prices with out carbon taxes.

Trump speaks the truth and no one else has that kinda juice--we need him: tell the youth!

We're stupid, were afraid, we have no vision. The whole culture's degraded so Jesus, start fishin'.

The animating contest is when you become your best fighting for liberty--it's your test.

Before fighting for liberty, I was a worm--needed approval from evil people/rebuff made me squirm.

Trump will fix it, understand that. Those others are no-where compared to the King Brat.

To me the biggest result of liberty is privacy. To not be invaded by messers causing anxiety.

INCOMPETENCY AND ABUSE: LIBERAL OBTUSE

VA heads responsible for incompetency and abuse. I know the crap that went on there and it's obtuse.

Donald, we just love you. You give us hope, man--we're so tired of the lascivious liberal crew.

WE'RE NOT ALL ONE

I used to be a liberal: no boundaries, lines nor morals too. That's the liberal mindset: pee-yoo.

Why can't they go back to Syria after Putin clears out vermin? If they stay, we die especially our women.

False Christians are idiotic, saying "peace" to enemies when true victory comes from fighting.

Obama paid Iran 150 billion dollars to build nukes but vetoed spending for the troops. Oops.

Liberal feminists think if you don't agree with them, you don't count. It's "The View" you must discount.

It's the animating contest for your liberty once you see the social chicanery of the peanut gallery.

Unless they believe it in heart, Christianity seems absurd--thus persecution across the world.

Demands of social justice warriors have become SO absurd they're a joke—remove this yoke!

Went to FOX, how boring. They omit or plain out LIE so I have 10 hrs found time, spirit soaring.

It's a mind-control cult so watch out. It's insane--makes no sense--but keep to truth/have no doubt.

Constantly lowering the standards and dehumanizing the middle class: conquering through sin, fast.

Dictators hate the poets. They always target them cuz they cut to the chase so you know it.

The silly students whine and scream as their "safe space" of not being offended is lamented.

Vindictive protectiveness describes the end of free speech on campuses by asses.

WE'RE NOT ALL ONE

Liberals vs. conservative hatred is growing: "affective partisan polarization" unknowingly.

Any firings will only encourage the mobs of our university's mentally ill, from false theories instilled.

Veterans: Thank you for your service though the country's gone left and they're banning our weapons.

Whoever's for socialism (Bernie Sanders) or Lewdism (Hillary Clinton) kindly leave (unfriend).

WE HATE EACH OTHER: STRICT DIVIDE

We hate each other: the left vs. the right. We see them as dumb, cold and vile so we must fight.

Conservative Christians are targeted in schools, families and trust funds: persecution is NO FUN.

They wanna break us down and make us obey: accepting their insanity in dismay--a world so grey.

Egotistical brats wanting attention. One day in the spotlight and now no mention?

Liberal illogic comes from finding moral equivalence between unequal forces--they justify asses.

Stay away from FOX news cuz they're not telling you the truth. Stick to the internet, be a sleuth.

When Muslims attack the left attacks victims: "Stop blaming Muslims and take a look at yourselves"

PC word battles instead of seeing clear and present danger. Could the students get any stranger?

The left's a pathological hex. The enemy is killing us and their chief concern is destroying/blocking critics.

WE'RE NOT ALL ONE

Evil brattish children are being used to take us into extreme Pol Pot tyranny. You talk and they get leery.

Such a breath of fresh air leaving liberal bastion California, despite it's beauty and how it warms ya.

If it's the left call them out and pin them down. It's the left--say that always about the clowns.

There are many heteros who want to adopt but the sick liberals would rather abort.

Conservative principals are best for lifting women up--for women need freedom: fill thy cup.

We're told not to stereotype but we can and we MUST do it to carry on this lethal fight.

PATHOLOGICAL ALTRUISM AND VIRTUE-SIGNALING

Pathological altruism: It's liberals and the churches who facilitate invasion by leeches.

How can you say we're like them! This shows your cold ignorance and lack of empathy, man.

Colorado College just banned the words "Jesus, God and Lord": You just can't say these words.

Alex Jones is a brilliant genius of this generation. Haters just don't like the vital information.

One disaster after another, frenetic: It helps to see it as prophetic in order to not panic.

Trump divided families on Thanksgiving Day. Many had to leave the table they felt so betrayed.

The entire generation lost how to think and the results of such mind-control will be a permanent stink.

WE'RE NOT ALL ONE

We have the first amendment in this country no matter what the crazy college kids say.

Ignore the movie stars, for liberals are being shown for all the filth and deception they are.

This is a sick old hippy witch. They're all around and in total control as they lie (give you a pitch).

THE CRAZY SAY DON'T FEAR

They say not to fear cuz they don't now what's going on. Don't listen to these loud lemmings, hon'

You know what it's like to be a pariah--when you speak your mind (though refined) they show paranoia.

If guns are outlawed only outlaws will have them and that's how liberal logic is flawed.

You wanna take our guns while letting those in who want to kill us? In you there is no justice.

Conservatives say "kill" those wanting to kill us. With liberals "don't hurt feelings" is their focus.

The bible is about people standing up against tyrants. Not laying down but fighting/killing giants.

Whenever you feel lost, hopeless or sad, just think of Donald. Become one with his mission, be bold.

Those who think clearly see Donald was the only way out. He is so wise like an energy spout.

"He" means "mankind"--a nonpersonal pronoun. Not "he and she"--that's just plain dumb.

Students threw paper airplanes at me when they saw I wouldn't always say "he and she" but just "he".

WE'RE NOT ALL ONE

They celebrated immorality and persecuted righteousness. Blessings stopped and judgment was a mess.

Praise God! Trump was divinely equipped and in perfect health to be our next president.

By telling us not to criticize they crippled our thought and that's why all the lies we bought.

Felt like a stranger in a strange land around 'em. Couldn't take who they believed in, like Hillary Clinton.

Please help us Father, to make America great again! There's only ONE who can do it, amen.

CULTURALLY-APPROVED SINS

Maybe your sin is something the culture approves of--even promotes. You'll still get old/ugly, folks.

Liberals find moral equivalence between all things and that's how they cause trouble/let in thieves.

Trump babes are wearing "Hillary for Prison" T-Shirts. Also, minorities are recent converts.

The kids and their dumbed parents are Christophobic and to kindly Christian folk they are acerbic.

When the youth chasten free speech tell em to shut up. These commies wanna blow it all up.

There was little racism before our chief created radical divisions and it's all precursory to fascism.

2016: USA's best or worst year depended on elections: either prosperity or no more protections.

Trump is the only one. Minorities, women and even some reformed Democrats love him.

WE'RE NOT ALL ONE

Some had Hillary or Sanders-lovers in their own family. What a horrible thing to endure, truly.

Trump hires women and puts them in prominent positions. Shut up detractors, stop fishin'.

So some ex-wife reports him as "frightening" and they come and get his guns—she's getting even.

THE TERRIBLE GROWING TYRANNY

The growing tyranny is terrible. California confiscating guns without calling AND banning ammo.

The Green Movement is phony (meant to ruin businesses) while the elites get all the money.

We're all gonna die so raise hell then die! We've been conquered by evil but God can still defy.

Though things look bleak we are told not to fear so look up for your salvation/joy is near.

We the people did not buy their garbage. 2015 is dead--now we have risen up, refurbished.

The average person isn't dumb just an expert on stupid stuff--the artificial reality of TV fluff.

It's our responsibility to fight this tyranny. What they call "tolerance" is really waging war on stability.

The Animating Contest: is becoming your best through fighting for liberty (your own and for me).

The Founding Fathers were all about defending freedom against tyranny, with guns mostly.

The only thing standing between us and total tyranny is an armed citizenry--that means you and me.

WE'RE NOT ALL ONE

San Diego is so beautiful. But, the grid's gonna go down with gang activity all around.

Liberals don't care about people, only their vision of how things should be and that's why we're unfree.

Just when we need our weapons the most he sought to take them away? Americans felt betrayed.

Tyranny always masks itself--trying to "comfort": Those false words and propaganda from Obummer.

WE WANT FREEDOM, NOT ENVYIN'

There should be no more envy/competition between us. freedom is all we want, so let's discuss.

Just when invaders wanna kill us he wants to take our guns? With leftists we should be done!

The irony is it's the left which is violent. Like liberals in families who shun patriots with silence.

Liberal psychologists call you mentally ill and then take your guns. This is trouble: tons.

If you protect yourself you'll be a minority of one--everyone is stuck in normalcy bias--but you must.

It's about control--forcing them to see therapists if they dare disagree: This is tyranny.

Oneism is false doctrine sending you to hell. Twoism is divine relationship with your father, a male.

Deceitful assumptions of virtue: they are not what they appear to be.

You're not gods and goddesses. You're sinners so get offa this.

Watch as liberal feminists rat out their ex-es. They love to label and diagnose men as the sexists.

WE'RE NOT ALL ONE

The Bill of Rights doesn't apply if you're white, male and Christian. Imagine that: take it in.

For those with Sanders- or Hillary-lovers in your family: See the gravity and how embarrassing, chilling.

Tyrants target classes of people and that's why it is so serious as we're overcome with evil.

Imploding societies demonstrate an explosion of homosexuality–not judging, it's reality.

LIBERALS CAN'T SEE CYCLES IN HISTORY

Liberals refuse to recognize cycles in history--to them everything is always the same. Lame.

They've wanted to take the guns from the sixties and now they're in control: the old hippies.

Liberals are evil people. They're committed to sin and run in packs to kill, destroy and steal.

To liberals this is Obama's stealth: Let violent immigrants in then destroy our right to defend ourselves.

The worst police tyranny is killing your dog just cuz they felt like it--it's how SWAT teams do it.

The one thing to know is we are in the right. Right always wins, doesn't it? Now good night.

This isn't what we want--these elites furnished by globalists, creating wars and lying to all of us.

Evil liberals have been dismantling this country for decades. It's the world of the dead: Hades.

Here's another one for those who don't know what's going on: We're goin' down, down, down.

WE'RE NOT ALL ONE

You mean to tell me all my parent's friends happily married 50 years were actually "gay"? Yah, ok.

People are attracted to it because they're in the majority. That's liberalism--it's just polls, really.

If foe has an AR15 you need an AR15, obviously. Jesus said it about the Roman sword--get a better one, ok

The left wins whether republicans are in there or not. All through gov it's theft, backroom deals and rot.

No fly lists: If you're on the list the Nazis they say you can't travel--you're goin' to the ghetto.

BRING IN RADICALS TO ATTACK US

Bringing in radicals to attack us then taking our rights when we DO get attacked: tyranny facts.

The only solution to gangster government is open carry nation-wide. Pass laws or moral slide.

You collaborators who went along with this: You destroyed your future too by thinking he was cool.

Taking our guns, saying our kids belong to them, teaching us how to talk: the level makes me balk.

You don't even get the power but now you're supposed to go along with this and love it!

Soros, Obama, Hillary, Moore and all you other trash. We will not submit, expect backlash.

We need to end this nightmare era starting in the sixties. These dinosaurs need to die out, truly.

Slaves don't have free speech and slaves can't own guns. They're totally vulnerable--no fun.

WE'RE NOT ALL ONE

Obama's attempt to overthrow the country, aided and abetted by congress: These are facts, not guess.

You have no idea the pressure I was under having to adapt to liberals. It stinks what they think.

Scenario: 1. Trump surges. 2. Obama is threatened. 3. False flag. 4. Martial Law declared. 5. Guns taken.

The Right to Bear Arms came intertwined with individual liberty. Anything else is Tyranny.

Tyranny is terrible as they decide to cast whole groups in a net. Suddenly it's worse to be a vet.

DUMBED DOWN MEANS DANGEROUS

It's scary living in a dumbed down generation without vision and who only vote by name recognition.

Let me get this straight. He wouldn't fight ISIS, brought them here while taking our guns: of course we feared.

America wasn't perfect but at least we had ideals. That made us unique: freedom is the appeal.

FOX is bashing Trump! Reason enough to drop them cold, they're boring and will end in a slump.

The globalists raise taxes and exempt themselves. Then they take the guns cuz tyranny never stops.

Obamagration: Flooding our cities with criminals and Jihadists and these people were sadists!

The evil democrats lost and will never get in again! Trump was surging with the greatest win!

Every department has SWAT teams. They break in at midnight, kill dogs and wreck your dreams.

WE'RE NOT ALL ONE

Because they're cowards dems target the innocent--not militant jihadis or illegal immigrants.

By not impeaching Obama our nationalist apathy will legally aid and abet our cultural death.

Democrats: You don't protect babies--the most innocent and vulnerable of all? Get ready to fall.

People lined up to adopt these babies--not abort--but this dems in blood lust will always thwart.

They make fun of women--look what they do to Hillary Clinton. But of course she deserves it: vermin.

DENY CLIMATE, LOSE GUN RIGHTS

Deny climate change, lose gun rights! Are you kidding--while shutting down our lights?

In a nation who doesn't protect babies, why would they care that Bill Clinton raped so many ladies?

What's he gonna do to us next? For eight years we were under daily torture with the Obama hex.

Obama was taking over through the expansion of bureaucracies then making congress fall in with out mercy.

The impeachment committee found 44 criminal charges against Obama. Such was our daily trauma!

He's compelled to target us because we're weak by putting up with him and obeying such freaks.

Those who know about the crime of treason and do nothing are as guilty as the one.

The problem with American Individualism is we don't community-organize like liberals, progressives and pres.

WE'RE NOT ALL ONE

The traitor has already targeted you as his enemy. Now man up and fight back against tyranny!

There are 200 countries in the world and only 6 can defend themselves. Guns make us individuals.

America is an anti-rape culture. In history our women slapped faces with the slightest disrespect, for sure.

Thank you God for raising up Donald Trump so he can save the country after so much treason/treachery.

I'm done. As the Titanic goes down (though Trump could turn it all around) I choose being renowned.

America's beautiful but won't be when the grid goes down--toilets unflushed, trash not picked up: no fun.

CONSERVATIVES ARE INDIVIDUALS

Conservatives are individuals so the problem is: we don't community-organize like dems or ISIS.

We were so scared we didn't know what to do. Our leader told us all was great but we knew, not true.

Fascism: merger of government and corporate. It means tyranny which is destructive and morbid.

Patriots are persecuted and if we don't stop it it'll spread like cancer but Trump is the answer.

Taxes, fines and fees: that's the mark of Tyrannies and it all starts by giving stuff away for free.

Fighting for liberty is the animating contest bringing you to your best: Handsome/pretty with zest.

You gotta tell your sexual history to enter colleges now. Like a cult of perversity of Satan or Mao.

WE'RE NOT ALL ONE

We already know he's the worst guy there ever was, no need to know the rest. We're scared/depressed.

The good leader unites everyone while the bad leader divides them--he's always triggering em, amen?

Fox has failed. They're increasingly anti-Trump and anything good and decent they've derailed.

The career criminal Hillary Clinton has fallen like a rock. Praise God we're rid of hideous double-talk.

At first they all shun patriots but later when it's accepted and costs nothing they'll all join us/be buddies.

TOLERANCE HAS LOST MEANING

Tolerance is the oldest American principal, but not for that--unless you're a pervert or imbecile.

They're so wrong and we're so right this revolution of ideas will be quick like a thief in the night.

The liberal agenda: Safe space Orwellian social justice warrior new world order hell in America.

In the sixties hippies were called "loving" but now they're in power and it's tyranny (crushing).

It's a liberal worldview seeing all humans as deserving of rights even the most perverse: yikes!

MAPS: Minor Attracted Persons (euphemism for pedophiles)

Banned from twitter for right-wing views yet they're allowed to advocate pedophilia in youtube videos.

Pedophiles: Atheists disbelieving in good vs. evil so liberals never see them as truly bad people.

WE'RE NOT ALL ONE

Anyone buying the leftist line--even one little slogan--will be less than he is and not well-spoken.

The Age of Cowardice is coming to an end just as the Age of Men is beginning to return, amen.

Tyrants say anyone trying to promote liberty is a "terrorist" and it's this us patriots must resist.

When liberals hear "Nazi" they think "right wing". But Hitler was a liberal socialist vegan who didn't drink.

WITH DONALD WE RETURN FROM THE BRINK

Through Donald we can return from the brink. If you can't see the state we're in you need a shrink.

The message was: "don't mess with us". This was very serious as we faced terrible tyranny in the U.S.

The liberal publisher said "If we took out all the offensive parts there wouldn't be a book left"--complement.

The world's been waiting for a leader who speaks from the heart not phony teleprompters, for a start.

Dumb females love to rely on government. It's like their daddy since they've degraded real men.

Instead of modest sweet little ladies, women have become monsters listening to feminists so shady.

He was fomenting race wars, can't you see that? A true leader is a unifier not a dirty divisive rat.

"Trumpism": Expression of legitimate anger over American events and the belief only Trump can solve it.

Liberals have nothing to say, they're empty. It's all talking points, party lines and whatever's trendy.

WE'RE NOT ALL ONE

The 5-4 SCOTUS majority was the only check on the left's gov expansion to take all of our property.

From London to New York people's heads are down, terrified. That's what happens with lost pride.

America: This leader has beat us up daily and many feel chagrin. You must feel big and proud again.

Revitalization Movements led by one with charisma bring sudden reversals--prosperity in America!

God help us, the country's been betrayed! But we can still come back if enough of us prayed.

LIBERAL MEANS GROSSNESS

Adapting to liberal culture brings grossness. A grossification of America has occurred, replacing greatness.

They get upset all day about things that don't matter. That's the left and feminists lost in chatter.

It's never been so urgent for men to find their male side (the animus) by rising up (despite feminists).

People are waking up in huge numbers! Thank you God for opening minds previously encumbered.

Your job is to show the world God--how He's way higher than the mob of liberals and other slobs.

For decades leftism has meant destruction under the veil of "loving tolerance" but it is the devil.

God raises up leaders at the perfect time. They're perfect for the job and defy the party line.

All through history are revitalization movements. Always led by a charismatic One—this is it.

WE'RE NOT ALL ONE

The man: The One who can bring it all together, from coal mining to feminist wives under the weather.

If you're against guns (the great equalizer) you're not a feminist and want women to be defenseless.

Just for speaking truth they'll call you "mean"--having adapted to the smiling phony fiends.

We're winning the information war: People waking up to this crap so fast and it's opening all doors!

FOX News is as bad as the rest--stealing the narrative and throwing it in your face--but it's collapsing, alas.

FOX is just Collaborators Stealing the Narrative, so ban it while seeing the falsehood of it.

FAKE NEWS LIES

This is how the news lies: not just by omission but framing things in certain ways--days in a daze.

History is being made. The media establishment is collapsing before our eyes and it's clear they lied.

Ignore 99% of what you hear. This gives you much found time--it's exhilarating, dear.

Don't be weak in front of other men, they may drug you. That's help-seeking in the wrong avenues.

Just the proportion of trivial vs. important news is a way of lying: It's how you frame it darlin'

Now is the time for all good men to come forward to the center: We're calling out all inventors!

Realize how different you are having standards, ethics and morals--and be alert/ready for scoundrels.

WE'RE NOT ALL ONE

Confirmed: Rubio was in bed with Murdoch at Fox. I tell you this backdoor manipulation just sux.

Banned means banned. When someone shows their obvious bias you must reject and nothing less.

In joking against Trump, Cruz made a complete fool of himself and fell like a rock. Genius is: Trump.

After eight years of extreme anguish we deserve a vacation. Work for Trump with community organizin'.

Eight years we've endured extreme anguish as we saw our country dismantled and bashed.

TRUST VERY FEW

Trust very few and decide who they are. Stop getting hurt by tolerance now proven wrong by far.

He wanted to kill us in the time he had left. Here are the consequences to elections: poverty and death.

Trump's an exemplar for the rest of us--of not taking any more crap after losing all our trust.

Many candidates are "limp handshakes" compared to our man Trump. Sense this then dump.

Though a puppet he's still to blame--selling our soul to the devil as millions see their lives leveled.

I didn't feel in the clear, he could do so much damage in under a year and we had plenty to fear.

The Lord has spoke! We'll get behind Trump and pray it's not a yoke but he'll make us rich not broke.

Every so often a Great Leader is risen up by God, His answer to devastating circumstances and fraud.

WE'RE NOT ALL ONE

God raises a genius to meet the need! That's due to His magnificent mercy: answering with speed.

Hillary and all the RINOS have tanked. It'd be good if they'd now go Trump for the highest rank.

All FOX talks about is her emails all day, never pointing out her huge crimes which they hide away.

If Hillary gets in she's gonna move against the people and we'll be in so much trouble: evil.

We can't stand to see his evil face. His name is Destruction and we hate this liar, fraud and disgrace.

MENTALLY ILL WOMEN POWER-TRIPPIN'

Mentally ill women into power-tripping with cult leader mommy Hillary: I have them in my own family.

It is not our government--just a bunch of cronies screwing us over and they're all phonies.

Hillary/RINOS tanked when fraud stepped in (that's always how they do it) but Trump's a shoe in.

Dam dems please leave cuz (you're for evil things and) you always have fraud up your sleeve.

Trump wants to be Geo Washington so let him! He's the only one not-bought and history will love him.

The New Age, medicine and feminism make a mockery of sex with prying questions--it's a hex.

Sex is sacred but the glib and casual way they talk about it is so embarrassing--shut up!

Yes, Bush was terrible but nothing compared to Obama. America's in ruins, we all feel trauma.

WE'RE NOT ALL ONE

Doctors: "Bleeding, difficulty breathing, trouble seeing--and BTW, How's your sex life?" (I'm unbelieving).

They don't come and take the guns, they infringe it on the edges--gradually we see the changes.

The founders said the feds are not superior to the states and the individual is sovereign--same weights.

OFFICIOUS DOCTOR'S QUESTIONS

The officious lascivious questions of doctors do embarrass, are needless and come from feminists.

We must eliminate the excessive use of force--whether we agree with victims or not, of course.

Trump is Scotch: Our brave heart is about freedom and shrewd business deals in God's kingdom.

Fox repeated "Marco Rubio's on a Surge..." Not true, it was Trump they sought to submerge.

They make out like bandits and the worst part is we've allowed it by our nonchalance, so stop it!

They're crude, lewd with big fake boobs. That's new age taught in the schools by feminist fools.

Don't tell me Christ never got angry--he tipped over tables! We're told to hate evil and all else is fables.

The Nazis used mosquitos as bio-weapons to poison the foe. Bill Gates does this now you know.

FOX sux: "Cruz is surging and Trump is failing". It was just the opposite from what they were saying.

The democrats have moved so far to the left, away from basic American values and vital issues.

WE'RE NOT ALL ONE

The democrats are well-versed in dirty tricks: cutting corners, killing foes and calling patriots hicks.

Mad how I've wasted years on FOX--a total waste of time but it takes what it takes to see what sux.

The democrats protect devils. They are anathema both here and Europe--a stench in God's nostrils.

Liberals work to protect criminals who've robbed and murdered, yet kill babies--doesn't that make you ill?

CONSTRAIN ENTERTAINMENT

Constrain TV choices to Classic Movies and the History Channel. All else is waste--leftist and modern.

The great thing about being black is no one can call you a racist for putting down this present fascist.

Highly motivated people who love liberty--these are the Christians who desperately want stability.

Corrupt government does not want things changed so they hate Trump and want Hillary (deranged).

Corrupt government hates Trump cuz he's the only one coming against them/don't reject him.

Everybody but us—we the people--hates Trump cuz he can't be controlled by their evil.

Trump is the only one who can beat the system cuz he doesn't need what the system uses, amen.

Even as the media trashes Trump he surged and prevailed but they pumped the others up meanwhile.

Since when does the sanctity of life mean a war against women's health? Since libs said it: filth.

WE'RE NOT ALL ONE

The liberal "climate change style" of broad, indistinct and meaningless generalizations is boring.

They say to media heads: "Either do what we say on Trump or we yank your advertisers", yes sir.

They're giving millions of dollars to stop Trump. The media must do this or risk being dumped.

The power Trump has is at the top, the liberal misperceptions at the bottom (which never stops).

This is our country we're losing. Not a football game but the real deal--forever, if they win.

I turned on FOX to see what's happening. It was so boring, so nothing, such silly laughing...

OBFUSCATION NO TRANSPARENCY

It's not about outright lying but obfuscation and no transparency. For bad tactics have no leniency.

They plant audiences, then by their reactions try to shift opinions--by booing Trump's words and visions.

They're lulled into complacency by milquetoast media and all their friends think the same: seedy.

If their reactions to what you say are liberal, don't give em a thought cuz they're really horrible.

You know that patriot who was shot dead by the feds? He was my neighbor in Cane Beds.

Police targeting of black people is a blatant lie disproven many times but Beyonce uses it as lines.

Turned Fox on, just to "see". It was boring and chillingly empty--withdrawal from addiction makes us free!

WE'RE NOT ALL ONE

Rainbow, Black Panther: Halftime celebration of democrat social platform as if LBGT is the norm!

Democrat social issues: Teaching filth to our kids. How did this perversion ever happen—be rid!

Filth taught to our kids is called "values clarification"--but we never agreed to this degradation!

Imagine teaching pornography to five year olds! That's how Common Core ruins our households.

MORALITY MADE AMERICA GREAT

What made America great was our moral foundation. We need to revert back: Revolution!

'I've unliked your pages, deleted your songs and will never buy a thing from either of you."--ex-Biance fan.

How did we allow this filth to take over? We've reached our breaking point--it's about our future!

Breaking point: Separate from bad associations going along with this filth for they ruined our spirit.

The Super Bowl: when Americans unite to watch our game 'til Beyonce divided us (bad dame).

FOX was my addiction (I needed it more but enjoyed it less) since I'm a scholar but it was fiction.

Beyonce is as much a traitor as Jane Fonda was in the sixties. Dividing us is causing violence swiftly!

We now have hope. What a relief after eight years of pure hell, every day feeling unequally yoked.

The college students are sickeningly stupid, having been deliberately dumbed and brainwashed (twisted).

WE'RE NOT ALL ONE

The most twisted are called "intellectuals". They make stuff up and we're forced to accept it all.

Trump wants to give back to a country that has given him so much. He will fix things with a magic touch!

Gloria Steinem says feminists stand against Islam sexism? What a joke, they do not, Ms. Steinem!

The left's lawlessness has awoken the sleeping giant of Christians demanding prosperity and freedom.

Rubio tast-tracked the TPP! What a terrible turncoat, and Fox wants this candidate, see?

Rubio is the front man for the Open Borders Syndicate. He's like a third term for Obama, let's face it.

BACKGROUND CHECKS LEADS TO CONFISCATION

Gun background checks will lead to confiscation which will lead to tyrannical government.

Trump is the only light in the darkness of theft, murder and debauchery. He is the only one, surely.

Arrogance is blindness and deviants are devious. That's why we hate these things: they're insidious.

The progressive left stands down with Islamists. Incredibly, this alliance also includes the feminists.

The soft liberals love tyranny and re-education camps cuz they haven't experienced the dumps.

You reap what you sow. You've left death/destruction from Libya to Russia—death to your soul.

Conservatives give more to charity than wealthy liberals. The "loving" leftists are often criminals.

WE'RE NOT ALL ONE

LIBERALS SIX TIMES MORE LIKELY TO STEAL

Liberals are six times more likely to steal while claiming they give to charity (but not = bad deals).

Gloria Steinem is an enemy of women and humanity. She won't expose FGM and Sharia law tragedies.

Hillary hired people to intimidate her husband's rape victims. And this you call feminist wisdom?

The west is the best place for women yet the feminists put it down constantly: I detest!

WINNERS SKIP DINNER
Waking up Refreshed and Fitter

OBLIGATE CARNIVORES VS. NWO VEGANS
LIFE IS A STRUGGLE ON POOR DIETS
MASS DELUSION OF VEGANISM
FROM FINE AND TALENTED TO PIG, LOOK AT ME.
LOW-FAT HIGH-FIBER SEVENTIES: TREACHERIES
VEGAN BRAIN FOG
THE SCOTCH LIKE MEAT WELL DONE
VEGAN LIBERAL FALSE NARRATIVES
VICTORY DAY WITH GOD YOUR PROMOTER
A LIFE'S WORK COMES TOGETHER
NOTHING "OUT THERE" AS INTERESTING AS MIND
LOOK OUT WINDOW: MUSE, THINK
THINK OF YOUR GREAT FUTURE
THANK GOD FOR THE OBSTACLES
I HAD A BUMP ON THE HEAD
CLEARING OUT OUTDATED SYSTEMS
CHURCHISM BECAME SOCIAL AND BORING
DAILY FASTARIAN: ONE WAY OUT
HOME-MADE CANDIES: NO FILLERS
SKIP DINNER AND DON'T DO LUNCH
YOU'LL KNOW WHEN TO FAST
SEE NEW AGE PAGANISM AS A WHOLE
BAKERY: STARCH/DAIRY/FRUIT/NUTS OR CHEMICALS?
SELFIX: AUTOPHAGY
PEOPLE ARE RUDE NOW: "OLD"
PALEO POWER NOT VEGANS OF THE HOUR

WINNERS SKIP DINNER

If I eat **NO PLANTS** for the day I have no bloating, acid or fears--it's all gone mysteriously away. **ALL WE HEARD** from the crazy seventies was the necessities of fiber but then truck-in-the-gut maladies. Vegan restaurants are another scam, too much sugar and fractured oils so you end up sickly not slim. From my death bed I punched in "ex-vegan" then all the info I needed, so happy I had to lie down/relieved. When I resumed childhood diet (even frying it) the whole world opened up to a glorious future/I'm living it. Vegans are always inventing "fake meat". Strange how they do this after screaming they hated it. Respiratory, breathing problems: Ended on a nebulizer. Social problems: ended in isolation as a hungry loner. Vegan blogs all discuss brain-fog. Wonder why--could it be the brain needs fat as it's made of cholesterol? Vegan **BLOAT** and **GAS**. if you don't believe me, go to a vegetarian convention and pass out fast.

WINNERS SKIP DINNER

OBLIGATE CARNIVORES VS. NWO VEGANS

Ex-vegan mothers recall with sadness their kids being hungry all the time and beans didn't solve this.

I was a sweet kid as a meat eater. Then I went vegan to be "loving" but was angry all the time, a fighter.

As a vegan not only was I not alive, I'd get into deep depressions/even suicide tendencies as I'd cry.

As a vegan I kept eating all day long to solve something that only MEAT fulfills while all my dreams, gone.

Sugar raises insulin, veggies' anti-nutrients to not be eaten, fiber is like nails/rotten. What's left? meat and dairy melts right in.

We don't eat very often but when we do eat, it's meat.

Veggies = anti-nutrients. Grains/fibers: bowl of nails. What's left? Provision from our friends, animals.

Keep that raw dairy coming—it's the only thing that's working. Not gonna put plants in my gut/burping.

Morning smoothie: raw milk, plain yogurt, half cup macadamia butter, three mango chunks, ENJOY.

I dreamed of pot roast and was hungry all the time. Despite that I still denied myself due to animal loving.

WE'RE NOT ALL ONE

I had sadly low self-esteem as a vegan, deprived of what I needed to be ME—that's why I reckon.

When mom shopped it was about the best cut of meat. That was the center of the meal but now it's s--t.

LIFE IS A STRUGGLE ON POOR DIETS

Give up meat and struggle with everything. Nothing makes sense so you take superfoods/ANYTHING.

I didn't relate my misery to my diet. Of course I was doing it right it's for animals, let alone fry it.

Twenty years of forgettable underwhelming lackluster work all cuz I was eating a diet even unfit for jerks.

Veganism isolated me terribly. It wasn't just that I ate differently but my personality was quirky/prickly.

Meat-eaters smell sweet and can finally think but vegans smell like rotting garbage, they stink.

My main meal was chicken but when a vegan I just saw a bird on a plate and was instantly sickened.

It wasn't pot slowing us down it was the vegan diet--had we eaten right we wouldn't need the palliative.

Yes I do link fruit with meat. Fruit and meat: after chicken in the morning in the afternoon a few grapes.

Now it's all about raw milk. I love it in the morning with yogurt in the blender with nut butter/coconut.

After being warped, post-veganism it takes a while to eat animal but as health revives you'll want more.

After eating HUGE salads it felt like nails in the gut. Read FIBER MENACE to understand the vegan rut.

WE'RE NOT ALL ONE

Where does new age veganism come from? Basically it's the globalist plan to make us sick, dead or dumb.

It's the NWO: Suddenly we saw the American diet of meat and potatoes as idiotic and rejected it.

MASS DELUSION OF VEGANISM

Suddenly we saw mom and pop as deluded victims of poor diet and cruel for eating animals/we said it.

So on top of destroying our health in a dangerous test we lost our family members who resisted it.

We were left alone with our fruit and tofu, our only friends liberal feminists to go to and poor health until lacto.

Vegan animal-lovers will persist on the diet making em pist until nearly dead with deficiencies/a long list.

It took me 17 years after dire warnings about veganism to leave it for home base: meat for children.

Humans don't eat carnivores but pigs are herbivores. Jews are kosher but Muslims extreme for sure.

Go ahead, enjoy your fiber (truck in the gut) but leave us alone we wanna be happy and avoid that rut.

We don't have the enzymes to break down all that plant fiber. Truck in the gut, depression: "I'm a loser".

Even omnivores aren't healthy. Look around, they're puffed up like couches, not handsome or pretty.

In the good ol' days the bringer of the pot roast was king of the party but now it's a keg of beer/smarties.

Carbohydrates trigger stress in body and make us emotionally unstable. But ALL of that? Crazy, trouble.

WE'RE NOT ALL ONE

I felt so sorry for the animals I couldn't make the switch. But dying from deficiencies I did it, quick.

How efficient: bake a chicken breast, eat then work all day. Or: all that work, expense and hell to pay?

Huge bowls of raw salad: The fiber I ate in the days of trouble, illness, doctors and wishing I were dead.

Freelee makes vids on the food she eats. Lentils with potatoes in a sludge base/makes us wanna cheat.

Durianrider makes vids of the gorgeous chicks who exist on fruit. Don't let this influence you/stay astute.

FROM FINE AND TALENTED TO PIG, LOOK AT ME.

From a young expert violinist (the best) he now makes Youtube mukbangs of gluttonous food fests.

After living on fruit Nikocado Avocado eats everything in sight, but meat needs less to be happy all night.

Severe digestive problems/mental issues. That's my legacy from vegan years but now no more feuds.

Durianrider makes vids from Thailand eating fruit all day surrounded by fruitarian women dressed skimpily.

Men wanna go to Thailand to eat pineapple and bananas to be like Durianrider-- that's how bad it is.

The family wanted to lock him up but he called that persecution for veganism cuz he couldn't see the crux.

Has Freelee diminished, has she lost it? From scintillating good looks she's now pale, lackluster, apathetic.

Now they're down on me cuz I say "eat meat". I don't like it any more than you do but I must or stay effete.

WE'RE NOT ALL ONE

Colorful sweet fruit promises glory, fame and feeling good so we kept eating it thinking we should.

I enjoyed a half a cantaloupe yesterday, but I don't need a crate or truckload of them like fruitarians say.

They eat all day, mega-truckloads of fruit then "smash down" rice, beans, potatoes at night, ole!

Lacto-fruitarianism: Have a few mango chunks in your raw milk smoothie--now you had your fruit sweetie.

Moderation, penury, frugality: they never heard of that but if they had fruit farms and groves it would be ok.

If I eat NO PLANTS for the day I have no bloating, acid or fears--it's all gone mysteriously away.

LOW-FAT HIGH-FIBER SEVENTIES: TREACHERIES

ALL WE HEARD from the crazy seventies was the necessities of fiber but then truck-in-the-gut maladies.

Vegan restaurants are another scam, too much sugar and fractured oils so you end up sickly not slim.

From my death bed I punched in "ex-vegan" then all the info I needed, so happy I had to lie down/relieved.

When I resumed childhood diet (even frying it) the whole world opened up to a glorious future/I'm living it.

Vegans are always inventing "fake meat". Strange how they do this after screaming they hated it.

Don't know if I could do raw meat, however. But enough benefits have accrued from the cooked/esp. liver.

I got drawn in to eating 20 bananas a day and that's just for breakfast, ok? Gained 20 pounds/dismayed.

WE'RE NOT ALL ONE

Ex-vegans lose weight feeling great relief returning to truth cuz God said it's ALL good what you eat: whew.

Nonsense things like "if vegan you save 600 gallons of water--so don't make a scene about water waste, ever."

Respiratory, breathing problems: Ended on a nebulizer. Social problems: ended in isolation as a hungry loner.

The crazy doctor told me to drink "Ensure" and the other chemical-filled potions of the devil, I am sure.

VEGAN BRAIN FOG

Vegan blogs all discuss brain-fog. Wonder why--could it be the brain needs fat as it's made of cholesterol?

Vegan BLOAT and GAS. if you don't believe me, go to a vegetarian convention and pass out fast.

To "cleanse" ourselves we took green powders which stuck in liver. Via colonics a "green snake" was delivered.

Veganism is like cocaine: Tho' it never works we keep returning to the first time when it put us in heaven.

Every time I ate I went to sleep. When I arose I sought fruit again but it never worked to give me pep.

I felt so crappy they told me to drink vinegar and lemon. Temporary relief then back to my acid condition.

Mom said "just live normally and the problem will go away." Sadly I defied her which I regret to this day.

The vegan life is filled with CURES for the problem this life produces. Panaceas, pills, enemas, superfoods.

Present food life: Raw milk smoothies mornings then meat, later a few grapes and no more problems.

WE'RE NOT ALL ONE

I was absolutely deceived on what is healthy and what is not. It's about ethics while body turns to rot.

I was so deceived that even after dissolved bones/losing teeth I argued with dentist who couldn't believe it.

I broke ribs, knee and two arms over ten years. I asked why is this happening? It confirmed my fears.

Paleo science: Hunters were tall, thick boned/good teeth for life. Farmers were short, fat and short life.

THE SCOTCH LIKE MEAT WELL DONE

I can't go from raw fruit to raw liver, brain, heart or placenta. I'll stay in cooked meat, that grey area.

In the skinny fifties handsome men/pretty ladies had a little meat, a few leaves and stayed very happy.

How I stayed a skinny lady: chicken breast for breakfast and a few grapes in the afternoon happily.

Eat meat to be (all-day) high as a kite. It's not just about that but oh, my.

Durianrider says it's a good thing to always be drinkin' water and pissin', drinking water and pissin....

The fact you'd want to hurt a dog so he's equal to a pig makes me sick. You've a cruel heart vegan witch.

The Atkins insulin theory is just that--a theory. If you wanna have fruit with your meat go ahead it's ok.

I personally feel fruit and meat is a perfectly balanced diet. It's satisfying, delicious, frugal, elegant.

I weigh 103 pounds today. If only I had known before what I know now, losing weight is so easy.

WE'RE NOT ALL ONE

The loving vegans are so cruel. Their brains deprived of cholesterol, the very thing making the Self true.

A sweet lil' lady has a chicken breast for breakfast and bowl of grapes in the afternoon/skinny and cool.

Any man/woman is handsome/pretty with grooming and diet--but grooming leaves when we've had it.

Avoid the new age or vegan trap. Why must we get so deluded before waking up to our OWN MAP?

VEGAN LIBERAL FALSE NARRATIVES

Vegans/liberals believe what they want to believe in a logical fallacy here--one I was in for many deficient years.

It's holistic: either mind influences body or body the mind--like being rich helps to transcend/stay high.

You start to take pills for pain or staying awake and eventually hit a wall cuz it's WAY more than you say.

When you become fit and tiny the only clothes are Chinese and Korean but that's ok, I love them.

Couldn't live with my clothes, the biggest contaminator of the chemically injured. Just a few, the rest stored.

Veganism was the reason for the explosion of MCS: Multiple Chemical Sensitivities. Eat meat.

All carnivores eat fruit and leaves but the ratio varies. For obligate carnivores it's just a few grapes.

They don't call it "low fat milk" but organic milk that's been watered down. Get cream = that's milkfat, whole.

So easy with dogs now: Give em their raw meat in the morning and no more begging, the little darlings.

WE'RE NOT ALL ONE

The only right answer is to fix the slaughterhouses, not make us all sick, old, wrinkled and wasted.

I actually prefer milk-fat, or cream. But when we do eat, it's meat.

If you wanna start smelling like garbage, eat a lot of fiber.

VICTORY DAY WITH GOD YOUR PROMOTER

VICTORY is a day, hour and minute.

Separate = holy. God has you hidden under His hand until your time has come and that's the best, truly.

Don't freak out with depression just cuz you're alone cuz God's hidden you for now/before being shown.

If you love God He's the only book marketer/promoter you'll need--logical but hard for them to believe.

There are times of day and the **WINNER** learns to maximize his peak periods: at 2 a.m. I am most serious.

You can't just do whatever you want, need Christian restraint. Control yourself, get some class you hick.

ALL great success was based on early nightmares overcome so **WHY** must you painfully recall all of em?

Nothing produces everything. And everything (society's superfluity) produces nothing cuz it blocks creativity.

What was their mistake? As usual, it was revealing who they really are.

To make you the best God put you through the ringer. Take joy, thank Him for it made you a right-winger.

You were a diamond in the rough, yuk! God had to put you through all this to make you brilliant and tough.

A LIFE'S WORK COMES TOGETHER

WE'RE NOT ALL ONE

To have a LIFE'S WORK suddenly come together after so much stormy weather having to endure the fetter.

You went through that cuz you hadn't learned boundaries. Without that the world flows in, evil cronies.

Don't resent past traumas when you were still naive. They were necessary for advancement to believe.

STOP going back 20-30 years when you were still immature and that's why those sad events of tears.

What you learned: How you act brings on a backlash in fact and THAT'S why these memories go black.

How God works: You work your whole life/don't make a penny but He pays you MUCH MORE another way.

DISCOVERIES IN ALL FIELDS

I've read about DISCOVERIES in all fields. Whether art or science they have certain characteristics.

Discoveries fit synchronistically in history--they answer a dying need. They are God's gift to humanity: SEE!

First rule of delicious solitude: never argue with lunatics or fools.

You wouldn't experience these traumas now since you're mature, have borders and know who you are!

God knows it hurts to look back (when you were desensitized to sin) but see it was YOU creating pain/lack.

To delete painful memories, take responsibility. You were part of the mix-- admit it and be forgiven instantly.

To make memories depart, see your part cuz you were a sinner with attractions to Satan/not God's heart.

See your part then bad memories depart.

WE'RE NOT ALL ONE

What is the basis of all wisdom? Fear of God, firstly--then fear of man (the deceitful and greedy).

Forgive--let go of resentment--and the answer comes you've been searching for, in an instant.

You changed but it was the devil--he is that powerful but it's forgotten, all those people are dead now.

Don't say "karma" just say "consequences" to sin--it's the same thing but nails where you've been.

Losers sleep late but winners--BILLIONAIRES--have early nights/arise early so they are most ready.

NOTHING "OUT THERE" AS INTERESTING AS MIND

Nothing out there is more interesting than my own mind--that discovered I joyously delved deep inside.

It's the nature of humans: contradictions, mixed signals, duplicity and flip-flops/pharisaic reversals.

Due to conflict the sinner implodes on his own. He doesn't need God to punish him, it's written in stone.

There's something about him/her that I just knew wasn't right, cuz I heard it in church when I was five.

I can sense evil in the pit of my gut and you can sense it too--UNLESS your conscience is seared/blue.

The Creative Act is huge: you write the draft a hundred times and at the end you spit it out in segments.

Let God be your promoter! He's your Champion, He brought you here. Work then wait to be discovered.

Let God be your Champion--become little. In a roaring world full of competition and ego, get humble.

WE'RE NOT ALL ONE

Suddenly the past breaks down as you come into your own. Although it still smarts, treated as a clown.

Whereas you were dead to it, conscience seared--now you're so aware of it but relieved and rescued.

What's superiority? Independence. Like the eagle who is unique, independence is our greatest strength.

It's hard not looking back at the horror that prepared you for success. Don't sink in your swill--progress!

It's hard not seething with resentment when recalling cads providing resistance to your ascendance.

LOOK OUT WINDOW: MUSE, THINK

It's most important that you stop everything and just look out the window now. Let God fill it all in, wow!

Keep getting away from it/opening up. Take the END very slowly, it's your last chance to influence pub.

The END--completion--will take care of itself. There's an inertia towards completion/no more insults.

Take a mental vacation, you must! How can God in-fill if you're stuck in some groove or trackin' public.

Free lance EACH job. Don't assume your tech guy can do everything, things don't work like that.

Seven books on Amazon. The Lord said after seven He'd do something.

It's not that I'm never satisfied it's that there's a right and wrong way to do things, that's my pride.

Stop working (extreme focus/tunnel vision) so you may ATTRACT instead. Can't do both so relax/be LED.

WE'RE NOT ALL ONE

I'm giving my books away (Amazon is low pay) cuz God always pays me more if I tithe that way.

My fears multiplied, a paranoid stressed out soul. Difficulties handing bad situations, was I getting old?

How to get rich: Give all your hard work away then God pays you another way.

After working for years without a money hunch God gave me a beautiful house and other things, a bunch.

THINK OF YOUR GREAT FUTURE

You don't have to be in a lotus position to meditate, just sit at your desk and think of the future: GREAT.

Faith is belief in spite of, even perhaps because of, the lack of evidence. Richard Dawkins

It's so good for the elderly to have a dog but PLEASE make arrangements for after you are gone.

Prepare for mass attractions to true self (fame) cuz you're the key to something of great importance dame.

Stop worrying about it, it was all the devil and when you repent it dissolves cuz the past is variant/flexible.

Traffic sounds can be like a boxcar speeding to a concentration camp or a road taking you to bright future.

Forgiving without repentance is heresy/creates criminals. Over and again he learns you're amenable.

It's the Total Therapy of walking away gently and never thinking about em again cuz life's too short, really.

It doesn't mean you're unforgiving just cuz you never wanna see em again, just going to the next one.

WE'RE NOT ALL ONE

We think we know someone so well then we're blindsided by something we never could've predicted.

What's that in the road, a head? Think FUTURISTICALLY to transcend the present pettiness/be led.

I hurt, I cry. Then a pearl of wisdom shoots out and it's all resolved--it was God cueing the quip, then bye.

I can't argue anymore, I've done my part. Ten books/8 picturestrips is all I can contribute for a start.

Just can't have em around. Unless they've had that revolution in the soul it'll never work I propound.

Yes, a LIFE'S WORK is coming together after so much stormy weather and I feel I am in heaven as a skier.

THANK GOD FOR THE OBSTACLES

Pain makes you stronger, betrayal more intelligent, disappointment more skillful and experience more wise.

Such strenuous multitasking (e.g.picturestripping) builds IQ--increases intelligence, I'm sure of it.

Poor watch more TV. TV brings sluggishness, low self-esteem and lack of motivation so choose wisely.

Before His Time Has Come the superior man is blocked at every turn. Wait for that minute then come first.

I hate gatherings. I find them boring, intrusive or spiritually down-putting and I'm done with em.

I've done my part. I don't have to argue with lunatics anymore it's my words in books they can explore.

Now is the time to fly above/transcend them and refuse to answer any more of their lunatic questions.

WE'RE NOT ALL ONE

It's called fame--be above them! Don't get sucked in, hold your head up high and be impervious to them.

It is so highly brilliant but because it's conservative they'll throw it out/block it or reject it, acting flippant.

My new wonderful life started the day I decided to not answer their stupid questions or react to them.

I HAD A BUMP ON THE HEAD

Famous scientific discoverer withdrew from the social cobweb by telling em he "got a bump on the head"

I did my part, figure it out for yourself. I told the truth as I saw it and beyond that I'm just the magic elf.

I'm telling you turn everything off but you. Go deep inside to truth, the key for world success to accrue.

Stop watching political videos you know it all anyway and it's way beneath you. No repetitions/just YOU.

Can't start till I have that click in my head. When's it gonna be done? I haven't had that click yet, Dad.

The more they call you "weird" the more you know you're on the right path cuz their conscience is seared.

STOP tracking your brilliant God-given mind with political videos cuz compared to you it's extremely boring.

You reach a point where you completely leave the internet and that's when you make it therein so DROP IT.

See all thefts of your stuff as tithing. God will put it to your benefit (took it cuz you wouldn't give it).

With tithing you increase tenfold says the TV so if you accept being robbed also expect more from God.

WE'RE NOT ALL ONE

This isn't the fifties, you can't trust your neighbors. Just cuz they live adjacent? Don't be ridiculous.

So he's gone, so what--I've got seven up there (got the boulder up the hill) so now the rest are downhill.

Things turn cold after the job is done, that's just the way it is man.

The problem is he wasn't reliable at times--guess I just required more than he could give me that's all.

You're not avoiding responsibility by saying it was the devil because it's true but now he's gone and subdued.

Refined people don't get mad at the savages they just skillfully turn their wheel around to avoid em.

CLEARING OUT OUTDATED SYSTEMS

It was cluttered with your stuff/you were gone alot but now it's a happy home with fence and gate/locked.

Don't envy me unless you wanna do what I did to get here. But you're just angry I'm doing better.

Was I directed by "chance" or was it miraculous--a magic coincidence? In universe there are no accidents.

I am sure it was a result of his aneurism/brain injury because WEAK men often fall into pornography.

Why do wives of men (into porn) commit suicide? Cuz it's an INVASION of an alien reality while hers died.

I was dethroned in my own home and that to me was a sickening psychic scream, a victim alone.

Sense of evil was unidentified. Thought it was me--where had happiness gone? It was morality that died.

WE'RE NOT ALL ONE

One genius discoverer in history simply said "I've had a stroke, I can't talk". That's the only way, hah.

Whatever the obstruction--her, him, it--just drop em and then open to the infinite, no more boxed in.

NO ONE would let me work. They'd say they would but then get restless and interrupt/bother: a curse.

Housekeeper knocks on my door, something I abhor! Signs on front: "don't knock/email me" ignored.

Guess I need a She Shed apart from the home with a fence around that, but still they would find me, crap!

People were just an encumbrance, they never added to my life--what I needed for success was INSIDE.

CHURCHISM BECAME SOCIAL AND BORING

Churches in a small town bothered me to go to their boring potlucks--saying it meant I didn't love God.

I don't wanna go to your group and I've hated all that since kindergarten when I panicked cuz you're nuts.

Many ruin present recalling horrible incidents when they were weak and ruined by Satan's descendants.

But you must understand the fact you went through that proved you still had it to learn so forget about it.

Neurotic are in the past. Einstein proved there is no time or space--the saint sits in time collapsed.

After suffering/overcoming you're now a success--now stop thinking of the mess making you greatest.

Do not go anywhere without a bodyguard or friends as witnesses to everything you do and say.

WE'RE NOT ALL ONE

It's not the end, it's the beginning of the end. There's a crucial difference as Winston Churchill said.

Being read is all I care about or ever will. Otherwise what use is this life pushing a big boulder up a hill?

Thank you tech guys who helped me push the boulder up the hill--couldn't have done it without you!

Just make your books available then sit tight, get high, think futuristically in assurance they'll buy.

I've done it, I don't have to do anymore. But I will because it's my life making you see thru the whore.

Free of him, just be like you were at seven--amused by clouds, sounds but turned off by leaven.

Now nothingness. The more vacuous the more fertile. It's called fertile anarchy as thoughts are circling.

Someone will see it. Relax, as God is co-Creator He'll also be your Promoter cuz He is your Father.

Don't waste time promoting your work cuz it's Gods--just prepare/get ready for cameras/perks.

DAILY FASTARIAN: ONE WAY OUT

Eat whatever you want, it's only one digestive burn a day and it all goes through by mass evacuation.

When I eat it's the most calorically dense, a cowboy thinks of that. Levoy Finnicum

I don't look at em as "meals" but just ONE "digestive burn" and "exposure" then not one morsel.

Fruits and vegetables are the only real ant-acids since everything else causes it.

WE'RE NOT ALL ONE

The densest nutrition is in the greens so if you can't eat kale, get romaine and eat it every day.

Tho' you may eat chips the greens are a buffer and delete effects.

Never take diet advice from a pagan. If they're into tarot cards take your own advice/drop em.

Americans were very hard-working people. Not stay home around a juicer they had to eat and run.

I've never desired rabbit food. Just fill the tank, stop the pangs then get back to work, soothed.

They carbed up in the morning then worked all day. They had delicious fats with it too so don't tell me.

If you make it he may not eat it so just fill his fridge with the best ingredients.

If you can't lose weight you need more fats like butter--high fat diet will change your life altogether.

She mixes fats with starches, breaking all rules. That's cuz it's only one digestive burn, she argues.

No digestive fire, there it sits, body reads it as an allergen or pathogen and you've had it man.

Not living on rabbit food hungry all the time needing so much but starch with fat then no lunch.

A substantial breakfast is how mom said to eat so that's how it's gonna be and I'm so hunger-free.

Fat/starch delays digestion to the lower colon so all day long you're not groanin' and can work glowin'.

Mom was mad when I ate lettuce for breakfast not starting out on my best foot calorically dense.

WE'RE NOT ALL ONE

It's the American way: a big breakfast then work all day. Fruit or salad for breakfast? NO WAY.

The very idea that us hardworking Americans have to hang around a frig/juicer to get our nutrients.

Fuel the tank, fast all day.

Can't create with three meals in the gut.

How to lose weight: skip dinner, don't eat lunch. Just do breakfast, a bunch.

Bakery is fine unless it's false then you build a big body like a horse.

HOME-MADE CANDIES: NO FILLERS

Candy addicts: Get it outa your system then reject totally cuz it's all fillers not like the old days.

In all things it is canola oil, soy, fructose corn syrup, gum but in different proportions/flavorings.

Scottish Shortbread (butter/sugar/flour) is better than all those chemicals and oils, the main killers.

Fat acceptance is hooked to thin privilege as we cascade down to this cultural mental illness.

GMO causes massive cancer, deformities and gene drift but globalist monsters say "it's the best."

GMO side effects are just old tech, now new stuff's rolling out and we'll be even more bloated up.

Everything is the same ingredients in different proportions and flavorings and all illegal in Europe.

This isn't candy, it's chemicals. Candy is real: chocolate, nuts, honey, sugar, butter, flavor natural.

WE'RE NOT ALL ONE

Aborted fetal tissue (AFT) to flavorings is based on murder therefore it's a ritual sacrifice/avoid em.

Most oils created by God have an armory of defense against this and that, anti-everything that's bad.

Avocado oil much better than coconut oil--the one they see as gold.

Scotch ate shortbread or it stores well instead: 1/3 sugar, 1/3 flour, 1/3 butter and pinch salt.

SKIP DINNER AND DON'T DO LUNCH

Way to life: skip dinner and don't do lunch.

Read ingredients--it ALL has the same poison just in different proportions. Soy, corn syrup, chemicals.

It's ok to eat candy if it's real ingredients, a quick way to get nutrients and sugar (energy) deliverance.

Fast fish is composed of the same ingredients as bakery--poison, but Europeans get the real thing.

Don't tell em what to eat just point out the cheat and they find their own way back to the real treats.

50% of our food is banned in Europe--think of that. Americans are so unsensuous eating crap.

Grandma's cookies and candies were such energizers and always digested just right, outa sight.

Don't tell em what to eat cuz then you're a darn clique again, a liberal social club and dietary tyranny.

Man is like dogs, omnivorous. We can adapt to many diets so don't tell em what to eat just be selective.

Oatmeal, bread, butter, dairy, eggs and bacon: Just a normal breakfast for centuries with Americans.

WE'RE NOT ALL ONE

Her grandad was a centenarion living on buttered popcorn and beer--re: diet, we just can't say for sure.

Her grandad was a centenarion living on buttered popcorn and beer--re: diet, we just can't say for sure.

We love shortbread cuz it makes us eat it otherwise we're not interested.

Eat, then that's it--it's all behind you. Now it's fasting consciousness, enjoy the luscious view!

Shortbread's used for Scottish armies or efficient fastarian satieties and is a cultural treasury.

YOU'LL KNOW WHEN TO FAST

Don't have to weigh, it's how my clothes fit: time to fast and feel legit.

Provide structure by a family breakfast, at least.

Popcorn is a delivery system for the butter.

Eat, don't eat, trip.

I have discovered the trick of fat with starch which delays digestion (satiety) for joyous fastin'.

Fats with starches allows eating less for satiety, delays digestion not hungry and flat gut, skinny.

I can take one digestive burn a day. Any more (to eat again) and it's all-night hell to pay.

Lotsa butter collapses calories (less eating) so you can happily go all day without food, flying.

Boil water, add Ramen otherwise tangerines are good for em.

One quarter of what you eat keeps you alive, the rest keeps your doctor alive. Egyptian proverb

WE'RE NOT ALL ONE

Two grilled cheese sandwiches, fast a day. It's gotta be calorically dense to live this way.

It's hard to fast 24 hours daily on one meal of fruit or salad. You gotta have more, then you'll love it.

Don't ever take diet advice from a pagan and soft porn is just as bad, though forgiven.

Go right for the superfood, like red bell pepper--it'll open up your throat and voice too.

SEE NEW AGE PAGANISM AS A WHOLE

Never ask a pagan witch filled with vice for diet advice.

Weight loss program: in the mornin' have bread/butter with jam then buttered popcorn now fastin'.

My parents ate butter--every meal and day--and stayed skinny that way.

How to love yourself and life better: Smother everything in butter.

Nothing is more delicious than butter and have you deprived yourself (of best food) believing nutters?

Not oils like canola, soy and all that lethal crap. But butter, the thing most loved by mom and dad.

When did cancer become epidemic? When we exchanged butter for lethal chemistry.

Parisian king opened his windows to take a deep breath of the morning air and got sewage/beware.

The chemically sensitive stop leaving home completely-- doing anything to avoid being sickly.

You resurface and they say "are you well now" cuz they don't know about total load--a sliding variable.

WE'RE NOT ALL ONE

By me not fixing food (slacking off) he becomes over reliant on candy for satiety/not good missy.

Walmart bakery is deliciously made from flavorings, soy, corn syrup and other poisons we gulp.

How could anything so delicious as Walmart Bakery be 100% made from chemicals? But it is, truly.

BAKERY: STARCH/DAIRY/FRUIT/NUTS OR CHEMICALS?

Read the bakery label--it should say fruit, flour, sugar and butter (different combos)--not chemicals!

It's simply shocking to eat a delicious cookie then belch with bubbles and acid all night and day.

Dive into the pies and cakes first then end the day with the best not the worst now fast/end curse.

The men were so handsome and the women so pretty and it's not just the food it's all toxicity.

Everyone looked so good in the fifties before there was fructose corn syrup on all things.

Start with acid end with alkaline that's the only way assured you won't have acid reflux at night.

Acid then alkaline, just skip dinner every time.

I solved the problem, no more acid at night. Acid am, alkaline noon, skip dinner, sleep tight.

Lifelong heartburn, gone. As me how.

Acid morning alkaline noon just skip dinner see me swoon.

Acid foods: breakfast goodies like pancakes, french toast, omelets, lotsa butter/starch/sweet.

WE'RE NOT ALL ONE

Alkaline foods: fruits/veggies/roots. Stick to that for noon now just skip dinner: thin as flute.

No I don't wanna go to your picnic and be attacked by flies. I wanna stay home and be amaze

SELFIX: AUTOPHAGY

In the desert I lived on dates—easy, no cook, satiety, sugar for energy, a fruit but dense, see?

There's times I'm into fats like nuts but it was fruit and starches some days just to fill up.

I eat to fill the tank so I can work all day and night but I love to fast, it's outa sight.

Plants nutritionally dense but not calorically dense so gotta keep eating em— no thanks.

I dreamed of pizzas ex-cheese, French toast w/ butter (much as pleased), decadent buffets, geez. -Vegan

It's just terrible: Anything processed/they're trying to kill us.

Make your own: Potato salad etc. in stores is filled with soybean oil!

Nutritional density means high water and low calories. No, I want satisfaction so I'm not hungry.

I'm down on nutritional density and UP on caloric density for the long haul-- high as a kite/having a ball.

PEOPLE ARE RUDE NOW: "OLD"

People start calling you "old" and you start to decline. Instead, live every moment until you die.

It's not the fact you're old but that they'd say it! Ageism is worse than racism but autophagy will cure it.

WE'RE NOT ALL ONE

When we don't eat the body eats itself--as inner spaces clear you now have cheekbones/hit on right combo for once.

It's a matter of filling the tank so you can get to work all day with glory to God and it's Him you thank.

PALEO POWER NOT VEGANS OF THE HOUR

So easy with dogs now: Give em their raw meat in the morning and no more begging, the little darlings.

The only right answer is to fix the slaughterhouses, not make us all sick, old, wrinkled and wasted.

I actually prefer milk-fat, or cream. But when we do eat, it's meat.

Fiber's like a bowl of nails to me. Very boring too, not where the flavor is--the fat God made for thee.

First I ate meat but then my tastes swerved to nut butters and creams. So what it's still fat/soft skin.

Butters and creams--that's how I ended up. High fat but low on the actual flesh cuz I love em all.

Fruit, butters and creams. Seems higher to me and I feel really cosmic and it's still far less eating.

Just fruits, butters and creams. Had some seed butter today and six hours later still no desire to eat.

Said "organic milk" but what a joke, so watered down it made us sick. Raw cream, it's the fat that works.

Meat had meaning at first but suddenly no logic to the system then fruit and fat worked/I reversed.

Sometimes I'm not into meat, don't know why. I made the mental switch/just prefer cream/fruit tonight.

If you wanna start smelling like garbage, eat a lot of fiber.

WINNERS SKIP DINNER

Betrayal Trauma hurts but you bury it just to do your work. It creeps back though, like a curse...

Read the 80 KK Books on prideful puffed-up powers and petty pugnacious peer politics.

THE HERD IN WORDS
HIX POLITIX
HOW THEY RUINED US
JUST SKIP DINNER
LE FEMME AND THE COMMUNIST SPIRIT
LIBERAL CHAOS & ROT
LIBERAL DOUBLETHINK
LIBERAL GALL 1 & 2
LIBERAL SHOVE-DOWNS
LOCK YOUR GATE
MANUAL FOR SUPERIOR MEN
MODERN ART FROM HELL
MOSTLY FAKE
NOTES TO CHAMPS 1 & 2
OVERCOME FRENEMIES
PC MAKES US CRAZY
PEOPLE ARE CRUEL
PEOPLE PROBLEMS 1 & 2
PERSECUTED GENIUIS
POLI-PSYCH MYSTERIES
PRETENTIOUS SLOBS
QUEEN BEE
RETURNING TO FIRST NATURE
THE SCHOOLS SCREWED EM UP
SEASON OF TREASON
SEPARATE MEANS HOLY
SOCIAL HYPNOTISM
SOLITUDE SOLUTION
SUPERCILIOUS
TOAD TO PRINCE
TRIALS CYCLES
TRUMP VS. GROUP
TRUST IN TRASH
THE TRUTH ABOUT PEOPLE
UNDERHEANDEDLY CLEVER
WALK TALL WITHIN WALLS
WE'RE NOT ALL ONE
WINNERS SKIP DINNER
WORK OR SMERK

AUTHOR BIO

Karen Kellock Ph.D.

Ph.D Political Psychology, UCI 1976
Post-Doctoral: UCI Medical School
Department of Psychiatry
Grants NIMH, NIAAA

Ph.D. dissertation "A Systems-Theoretic View of Pathologic Interaction" made an early mark as the "Wife of the Alcoholic Syndrome". Postdoctoral research at UCI Medical, Dept. of Psychiatry on the systems surrounding pathology on NIMH and NIAAA federal grants: *The Contagion of Madness: The Psychology of Neurotic Interaction and Pathological Systems*. Therapy tool Therapeutic Playwriting introduced the play *Mary and Murv: Gruesome Twosomes in the Alcoholic Marriage*. She taught Abnormal Psychology and Pathological Systems Theory at UC and CSU campuses and developed "the Debris Theory of Disease" in five books and website: (www.karenkellock.org): *Champion Guides, Daily Fastarian, Just Skip Dinner, Arts of Paleo Fasting, Ageless Cornucopia. Manual for Superior Men is a* pick-it-up-anywhere book that you can't put down (20,000 Kellockialisms) and ever on your desktop it should be found (or this Ebook for superior wordsearch of new jargon).